Now I Know

Our Friend the Sun

Written by Janet Palazzo
Illustrated by Susan Hall

Troll Associates

Library of Congress Cataloging in Publication Data

Palazzo, Janet.
    Our friend the sun.

    (Now I know)
    Summary: Simple text and illustrations introduce
the characteristics of the sun and its relationship
to the earth.
    1. Sun—Juvenile literature. [1. Sun] I. Hall,
Susan, ill II. Title.
QB521.5.P34   523.7   81-11460
ISBN 0-89375-650-4   AACR2
ISBN 0-89375-651-2 (pbk.)

10   9   8   7   6   5   4   3

This pretty flower has a friend.

This little butterfly has a friend.

These girls and boys have a friend.

Who is their friend?

Can you guess?

This is their friend—

the sun.

Sunshine helps the flowers bloom.

Sunshine helps the grass grow tall.

Sun makes the earth a home for us all.

The sun is a star.

It is our special star.

The sun gives us light.

It gives us heat, too.

Do you know what else the sun can do?

It helps us tell time.

Is it morning, noon, or night?

It's morning now. It's time to rise.

Now it's night—close your eyes.

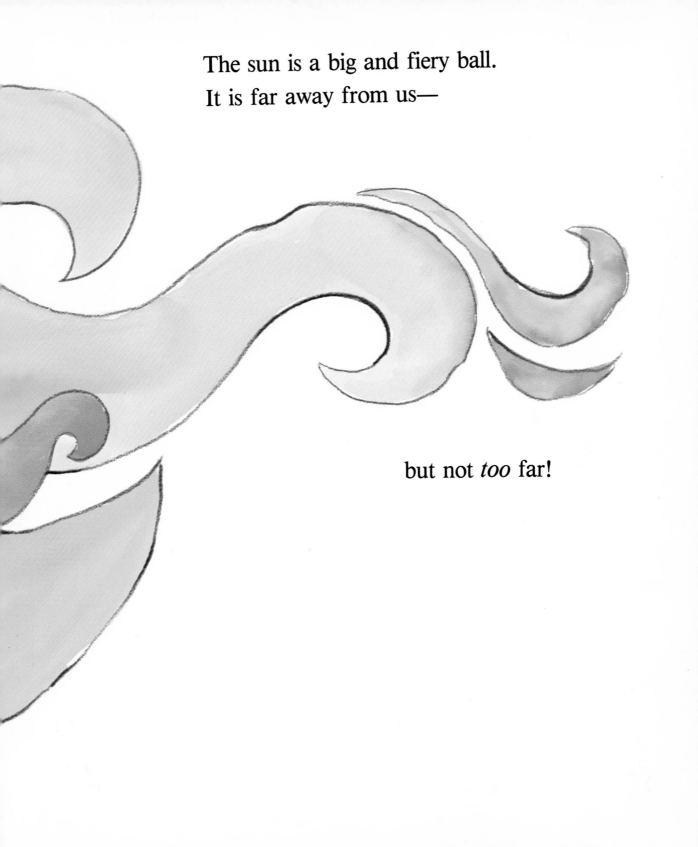

The sun is a big and fiery ball.
It is far away from us—

but not *too* far!

If the sun was too far,

we'd be too cold.

If the sun was too close,

we'd be too hot.

But our special star is just far enough.

It's just far enough
to help things grow—

like animals, flowers and trees,
and you and me!